An Heirloom Book of

The Nativity

Presented to

Kathleen Munson

by

Mrs Sophie Young

12/25/1990

An Heirloom Book of

The Nativity

by

MARCEIL FLEMING LETTS

and

BEVERLY ALSTON QUINLAN

Illustrations by

KENNETH SPENGLER

THE HEIRLOOM BOOK COMPANY, INC.

Morris Plains, New Jersey

THE HEIRLOOM BOOK COMPANY, INC.
6 Glencove Road
Morris Plains, NJ 07950

Library of Congress No.: 89-080890
ISBN 0-9623558-0-1

Printed in West Germany

DEDICATED TO:

Our young

Ian
Diana

and our not so young

Cecelia
Virgie
Walter

REMEMBERING

Robert

WITH THANKS TO
Howard & Sean

Barbara	*Billy*
Eric	*Susan*
Kimberly	*Catherine*
Mary Pat	*Martha*
Virginia	*Vivian*
Glen	*Paul*
Patricia	*Claude*

Monsignor Frank Ferraioli

Table of Contents

"For God so loved the world that
He gave His only begotten Son,
That all who believe in Him
Shall not die, but have eternal life."
—JOHN 3:16

Foreword

CHRISTMAS IS A TIME *of great festivity. Much planning and preparation is done for this day as well as for the many other celebrations throughout the holiday season. Gifts are purchased for friends and loved ones, homes are decorated, parties are held, cookies are baked. It is a very busy time.*

Finally, the day arrives. Families gather, gifts are opened and wonderful meals are eaten. Then the day is over. The decorations are packed away for next year and the merriment of the season is soon little but a dim memory. All too often, there is left a sense of emptiness and lack of fulfillment.

Perhaps had time been taken to ponder the real meaning of Christmas, the spirit of the day would have been lasting. Had thought been given to the birth of Christ and what that represented to the world, then the joy and hope experienced by people for centuries would have remained long after the festivities were over.

Remembering the true meaning of Christmas is what this book is about.

We began writing "The Nativity" one year after having shopped unsuccessfully for a book of this type. We were looking for a book to give to friends and family that would encourage some quiet and thoughtful reflection during the holidays. We wanted an attractive, intelligent presentation of this wonderful story that would be appropriate for all, the young and the not so young. We wanted something that parents could share with their children, that the children would enjoy on their own as they grew and, in turn, pass on to their children. Not finding such a book, we wrote our own.

We hope you enjoy reading "The Nativity" as much as we have enjoyed writing it. We hope that the presentation informs you and the illustrations please you. But most of all, it is our wish that this book will help make Christmas a holy day, as well as a holiday and that you will experience a sense of joy and hope for Peace on Earth and Good Will Toward Man.

An Heirloom Book of

The Nativity

⁂

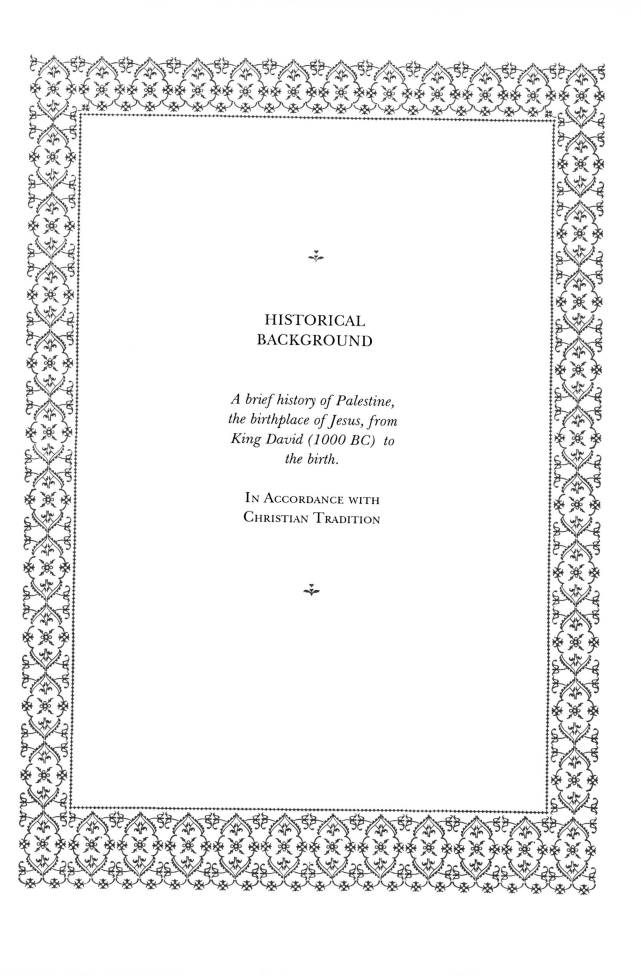

HISTORICAL BACKGROUND

A brief history of Palestine, the birthplace of Jesus, from King David (1000 BC) to the birth.

IN ACCORDANCE WITH CHRISTIAN TRADITION

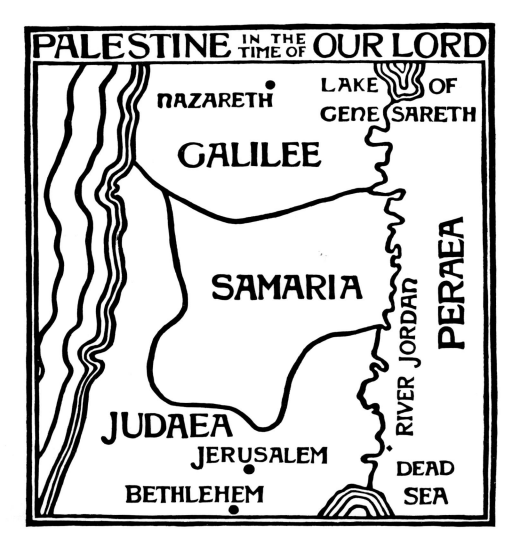

This map is printed with the kind permission of
the Abbaye de Saint-André, 8200 Bruges, Belgium.

[2]

Historical Background

J ESUS WAS BORN AND LIVED in Palestine, most of which today is the country of Israel. Palestine, at that time, was divided into four provinces: Galilee in the north, Judea in the southwest, Samaria in the center and Perea to the east of the other provinces. The city of Nazareth, where Jesus spent his early life, was in Galilee. Bethlehem, the place of His birth, was in Judea. Often referred to as the City of David, Bethlehem still exists today and the Nativity is celebrated there every year.

In ancient times, Palestine was known as the Kingdom of Israel. David of Bethlehem ruled the kingdom from approximately 1000 BC to 962 BC. King David was a distinguished warrior and great political leader. He united the many tribes of Israel into a powerful empire with Jerusalem as the capital. After his death, his son Solomon, from his marriage to Bathsheba, succeeded him as king of Palestine.

Like his father, Solomon was a great military leader. However, he is better remembered in history for his ambitious building and trading programs which improved the empire culturally and commercially. Solomon ruled for about 40 years and, in his time, was considered to be wiser than all other men. Today, when the saying "the wisdom of Solomon" is used, it is in reference to this King Solomon. Joseph, husband of Mary the mother of Jesus, was a direct descendant of David and Solomon, with some 26 generations between Solomon and Joseph.

After Solomon's reign, the Kingdom of Israel was divided. Solomon's heirs ruled the smaller Kingdom of Judah until all of Palestine was conquered in succession by the Babylonians, Persians, the empire of Alexander the Great, the Ptolemies, Seleucids and the Roman Empire.

[3]

Palestine was conquered in 63 BC by the Roman leader Pompeius Magnus, or Pompey the Great. In 60 BC, Pompey and two other Romans, Marcus Crassus and Julius Caesar, formed a triumvirate to rule the entire Roman Empire. However, after several years, bitter jealousies arose among the three rulers and in 48 BC Caesar's armies defeated those of Crassus and Pompey. Caesar then became dictator over the Empire and ruled until his assassination in 44 BC by two Roman senators, Brutus and Cassius.

Following Caesar's death, his grandnephew and adopted son, Caesar Augustus, formed a triumvirate with Marcus Lepidus and Marcus Antonius, better known in history as Mark Anthony, husband of Cleopatra. These three ruled the Roman Empire from 43 BC until struggles for power and territory erupted among them. In 32 BC, Caesar Augustus defeated Marcus Lipidus and the following year overthrew Mark Anthony. Augustus then became emperor and ruled until his death in 14 AD.

But while Mark Anthony was in power, he supported his friend Herod the Great in his rise to leadership in Palestine. In 41 BC, Anthony appointed Herod tetrarch of Galilee and in 40 BC, sponsored him to be named King of Judea.

Herod was born in 73 BC, the son of Antipater, a wealthy and influential leader in Judea. Antipater had wisely established ties with the Romans after their conquest of Palestine. These bonds were to benefit his son, when, in 57 BC, Herod met and formed a lifelong friendship with Mark Anthony. After Mark Anthony was overthrown, Herod became an ally of Caesar Augustus. With the support of Augustus, Herod continued to gain power and, by 24 BC, ruled all of Palestine under the Romans.

In his later years, Herod became mentally unstable. He reacted violently whenever he suspected disloyalty among his family. This led him to have his first born son, Antipater, as well as his wife, Mariame, killed. He was also fearful of any threat to his power. Upon hearing of the birth of a King in Bethlehem, he attempted to kill Jesus by ordering that all male infants two years of age and under in Bethlehem and the surrounding area be murdered.

Herod died in four BC and his realm was divided among his sons, Philip, Antipas and Archelaus.* It was Antipas who would, several years later, take part in the trial of Jesus and turn Him over to Pontius Pilate for crucifixion.

And so it was during the reigns of the Roman Emperor Augustus and King Herod of Palestine that Jesus was born. Augustus, just prior to the birth of Jesus, had sent out a decree ordering that a census be taken throughout the Roman Empire. The purpose of the census was to identify who should be taxed and the amount of their taxation. All adult males were required to register in the town of their ancestors. For Joseph, that was Bethlehem, since he was a descendant of the house of King David. He therefore had to travel from Nazareth, where he lived and worked as a carpenter, to Bethlehem to register. Mary, although near term with Jesus, accompanied him. That is how Jesus, the Messiah, came to be born in Bethlehem.

---

*The system of reckoning years as before the Nativity or after, BC or AD, was defined by a monk, Dionysius Exiguus, in the sixth century. However, some 200 years later, it was discovered that he had miscalculated the year Christ was born. In the eighth century, it was determined that since Herod died in four BC, the Nativity took place that year or shortly before.

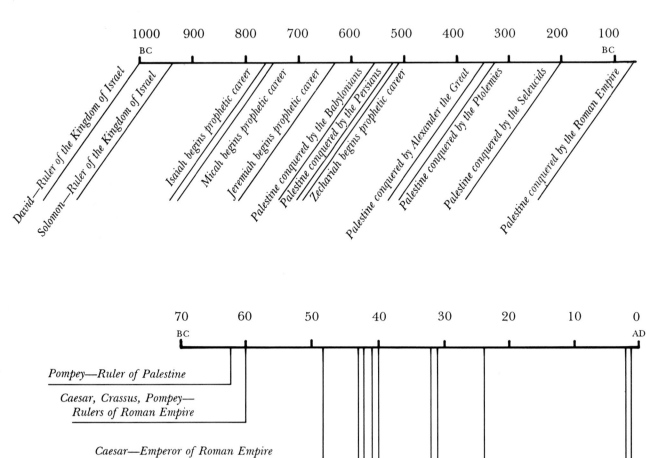

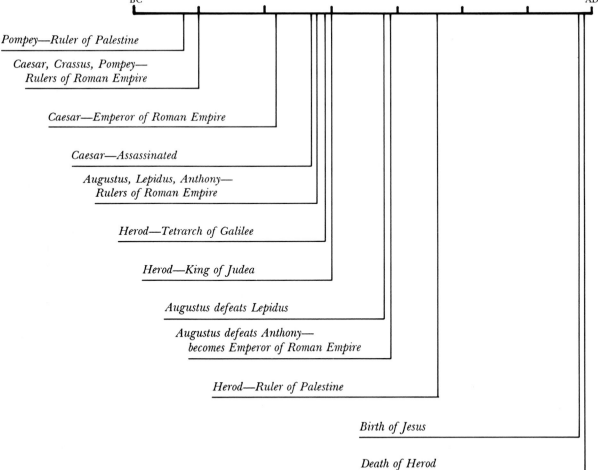

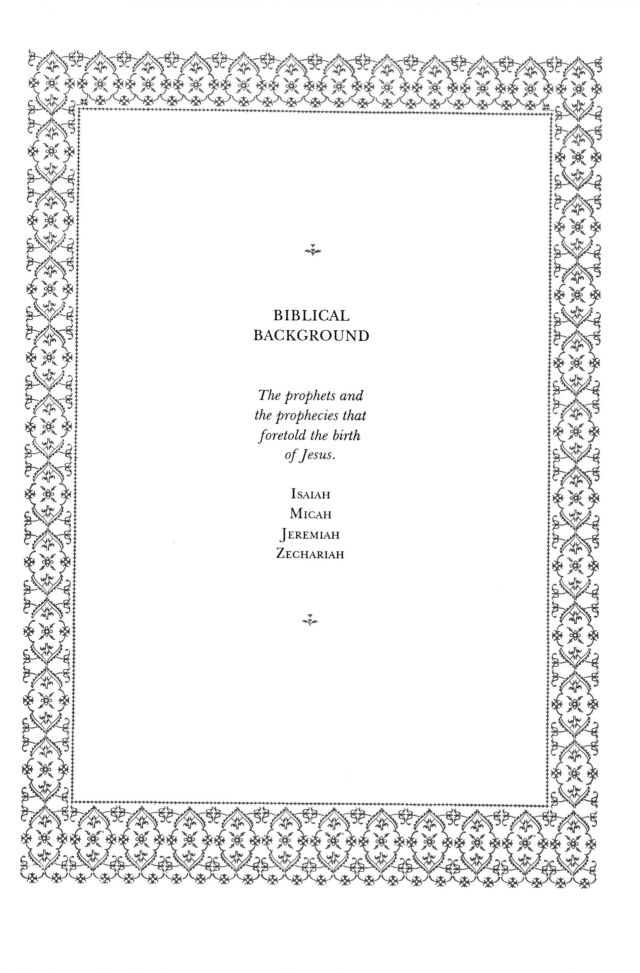

BIBLICAL BACKGROUND

*The prophets and
the prophecies that
foretold the birth
of Jesus.*

Isaiah
Micah
Jeremiah
Zechariah

Biblical Background
The Prophecies

THERE WAS A SENSE OF ANTICIPATION within the Kingdom of Israel in the days prior to the birth of Jesus. This might be difficult to understand, considering the turbulent history of the Hebrew people. For several hundred years, their nation had experienced a continual decline until this time when they found themselves ruled by the Roman Empire. Burdened with such a painful past, the Hebrew people might have succumbed to despair. However, they had a sense of hope and excitement about their future. Their optimism was in large measure due to the spiritual guidance and predictions of the Hebrew prophets.

The prophets had a very distinct role in the society of their time. They were the spiritual guides of the people during times of social and political upheaval. They dealt with the difficult political and social issues of the day and called upon the people to maintain strict adherence to the laws of God in the midst of these struggles. Their role was to "forthtell" what the law of God required.

The role of "forthtelling" or preaching the will of God had several aspects. The prophets warned the Hebrew nation of the consequences of disobedience, called them back to God in repentance and comforted them with the assurance that He would return to them with an everlasting love.

The prophets functioned not only as "forthtellers" of the will of God, but also as "foretellers" of the future plans of God. Their foretellings of events spanned four points in time: the current, the near future, the far future and the most distant future. Often, the prophets were unaware of the point in time to which a particular prediction applied, because the messages of God were not time specific.

The predictions of the prophets were not usually of happy events. Often they warned of impending disasters, either social, physical or political. However, many of the prophecies foretold of good times, when the Hebrew people would be free and peace would reign in their land. These prophecies of consolation often spoke of the coming of the Messiah as well as the circumstances of His birth, life and death.

Many prophecies of consolation are recorded in the Old Testament. The prophecies of Isaiah, Micah, Jeremiah and Zechariah spoke clearly of the coming of the Messiah. These were the source of hope for the Hebrew people, who patiently awaited their fulfillment.

The Prophet Isaiah

ISAIAH IS CONSIDERED the greatest of the ancient prophets. He wrote two prophecies predicting the birth of the Messiah some 700 years before it occurred.

> *"Therefore, the Lord Himself*
> *shall give you a sign.*
>
> *The virgin shall be with Child*
> *and shall give birth to a Son.*
>
> *And she shall call Him Immanuel."*
> ISAIAH 7:14

> *"For unto us a Child is born,*
> *To us a Son is given.*
>
> *And dominion shall*
> *be laid on His shoulders.*
>
> *He shall be called Wonderful,*
> *Counselor, Mighty God,*
> *Everlasting Father, Prince of Peace."*
> ISAIAH 9:6

Isaiah, whose name means "Jehovah is Salvation," was born in Jerusalem in the eighth century BC. It is thought that he was from an aristocratic family, since he associated with royalty and was well-informed about public affairs.

[10]

Isaiah was called to be a prophet in about 742 BC, probably in the Temple of Jerusalem. He prophesied mainly to the people of the Kingdom of Judah, of which Jerusalem was a part in those times. Isaiah attacked the many social problems of his day, not only because he was sympathetic toward the poor and needy, but also because he saw these problems as symptoms of spiritual decline.

The prophecies of Isaiah were both stern and tender. They contained messages of judgement and doom, as well as messages of great hope. His greatest message of hope was that God would send a Messiah to save His people and establish a kingdom of righteousness.

Isaiah prophesied for over forty years. There is a Hebrew legend that says he was martyred at the hands of the wicked King Manasseh of Judah.

The Prophet Micah

MICAH WAS ESPECIALLY NOTED for his predictive messages. His prophecy about the coming of the Messiah even identified Bethlehem as His birthplace.

"But you, Bethlehem in Ephrathah,
Though small among the clans of Judah,
From you shall come forth a Ruler,
One whose roots are from long past.

The Lord shall abandon His people to
their enemies,
Until she who is to give birth has
borne her Son.

He shall stand and feed in the
strength of the Lord,
And they shall abide in Him, for His
greatness shall reach to the ends of the earth.

He shall be a Man of Peace."
MICAH 5:2-5

A contemporary of Isaiah, Micah was born in the little village of Moresheth in the foothills of Judea, and prophesied mainly to the people in that part of Palestine. The name Micah means "who is like the Lord."

The messages of Micah were frequently directed toward the sinfulness of the society of his time. He attacked unethical merchants, corrupt priests and judges and the rich who exploited the poor. He warned the people of coming disaster if they did not repent, predicting the destruction of Jerusalem. However, Micah also spoke of restoration. He was sure that someday the Lord would restore Israel to a place of prominence in the world under the Messiah.

The Prophet Jeremiah

MOST OF THE PROPHECIES of Jeremiah were stern messages of judgement. But he also delivered messages of hope and restoration. In particular, Jeremiah prophesied about the coming of the Messiah who would save His people.

> *"Behold, the days are coming,*
> *Declares the Lord,*
> *When I shall raise up a righteous*
> *Branch unto David.*
>
> *He shall be a King who shall rule*
> *with wisdom and justice,*
> *And cause righteousness to*
> *prevail throughout the land.*
>
> *This is the name they shall give Him:*
> *'The Lord Our Righteousness.'"*
> JEREMIAH 23:5-6

Jeremiah lived almost 100 years after Isaiah. He was born about 650 BC in the village of Anathoth, a few miles northeast of Jerusalem. He grew up in a priestly family and in his childhood studied the messages of former prophets.

Jeremiah began his prophetic career in 627 BC while in his early twenties. He was, by nature, sensitive and sympathetic. Often suffering from periods of great sadness, he is sometimes called the "weeping prophet" or the "prophet of loneliness."

Jeremiah, more than any other prophet, spoke of the need for repentance. He denounced the people of his time for their wickedness and called upon them to reform and return to the ways of the Lord. Like Micah before him, Jeremiah predicted that God would punish the people by destroying the Temple of Jerusalem. This prophecy came true during his lifetime when the Babylonians conquered and destroyed all of Jerusalem, including the Temple, in 586 BC.

When Jerusalem was conquered, Jeremiah was taken against his will to Egypt by people who feared the Babylonians and sought to protect him. There, he continued to rebuke his fellow exiles until he died about 570 BC. According to one tradition, he was martyred by his fellow countrymen.

The Prophet Zechariah

A FREQUENT THEME in the prophecies of Zechariah was the restoration of the Kingdom of Israel. He foretold of the coming of a humble King, Who would lead the Kingdom to a place of prominence again.

> *"Rejoice greatly, O daughter of Zion,*
> *Shout with gladness, O daughter of Jerusalem!*
>
> *Behold, your King is coming to you,*
> *He is just and having salvation.*
>
> *Yet He is meek, riding on an ass,*
> *On a colt, the foal of an ass.*
>
> *He shall banish the chariot from Ephraim*
> *and the war-horse from Jerusalem.*
>
> *The warrior's bow shall be banished*
> *and He shall proclaim peace to every nation.*
>
> *His dominion shall be from sea to sea,*
> *From the river to the ends of the earth."*
> ZECHARIAH 9:9-10

Zechariah was born about the middle of the sixth century BC in

Babylon. He was a descendant of the Hebrews who were taken into exile when Jerusalem was conquered by the Babylonians.

When the Babylonian Empire fell to the Persians in 539 BC, the Hebrew exiles were permitted to return to Jerusalem and to rebuild their Temple. Zechariah was among those who returned to restore the Temple and to gather and preserve the sacred traditions of the Hebrew people.

Zechariah, whose name means "the Lord remembers," began his ministry about 520 BC. Many of his prophetic messages served to encourage the people in their efforts to rebuild the Temple and restore their nation.

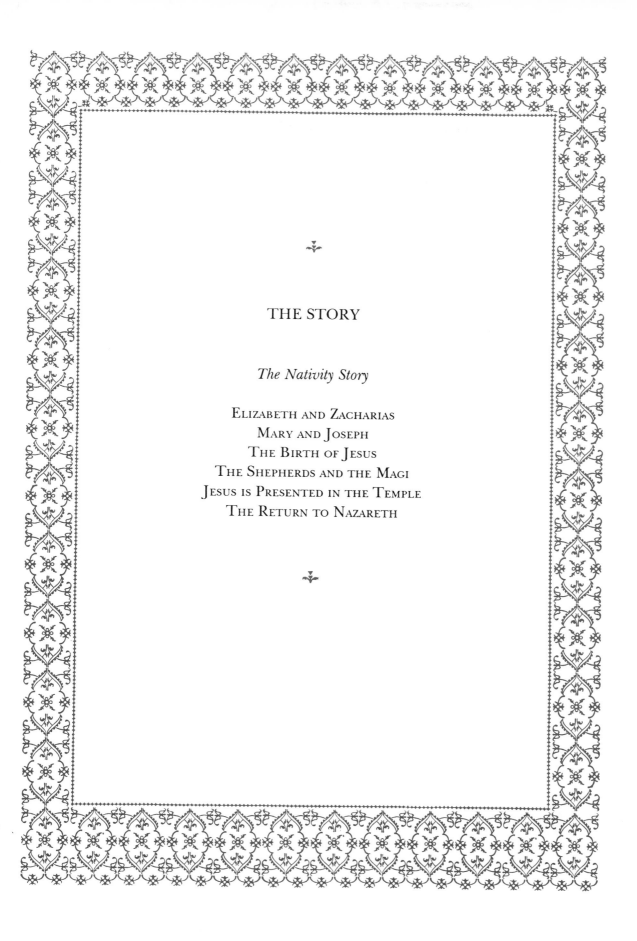

THE STORY

The Nativity Story

Elizabeth and Zacharias

DURING THE REIGN OF Herod the Great, there lived a Hebrew priest named Zacharias. Zacharias lived in the hills of Judea with his wife, Elizabeth. They were a devout couple, careful to obey all of the laws of God. Yet, there was a quiet sadness about them, for Elizabeth was unable to bear children and, now, they were both very old.

This was a hardship for Elizabeth and Zacharias to endure, for the people of that day believed that if you did not have children, you were outside the blessing of God. Although their prayers for a child seemed to have gone unanswered, they nevertheless remained faithful to God, and Zacharias never forsook his priestly duties.

Zacharias served in the Temple in Jerusalem, the only temple in all of Palestine. At that time, there were thousands of priests, far too many to serve in the Temple at one time. They were, therefore, divided into separate groups. Each group served on temple duty for two weeks each year.

The duties of the priests were to manage the upkeep of the Temple, teach the people the word of God and direct the worship services. Each morning, one priest was selected to enter the inner sanctuary of the Temple and offer incense before the Lord. This was an honor bestowed upon a priest perhaps only once in his lifetime since lots were cast to decide which priest would enter the sacred room.

One day, when Zacharias was serving in the Temple, he was chosen to offer the incense in the sanctuary of the Lord. When Zacharias entered the sanctuary, a multitude of people gathered outside the Temple to pray, as was their daily custom. While Zacharias was praying in the sanctuary, an angel of the Lord appeared, standing at the right side of the altar of incense. Upon seeing the angel, Zacharias was most troubled and fear fell upon him. But the angel said to him:

"Fear not, Zacharias, for your prayer is heard.
Your wife, Elizabeth, shall bear you a son and
you shall call him John.

"And you shall have joy and gladness and many
shall rejoice at his birth.

"For he shall be great in the sight of the Lord
and shall be filled with the Holy Spirit.

"And he shall turn many of the children of Israel
to the Lord their God.

"He shall go before Him in the spirit and power
of Elijah, to make ready a people prepared
for the Lord."

Then Zacharias said to the angel:

"How am I to know this? For I am an old man,
And my wife, too, is advanced in years."

The angel replied:

"I am Gabriel and stand in the presence of God.
I have been sent to speak to you and to bring
you these glad tidings.

"And, because you did not believe my words,
Behold, you shall be dumb and unable to speak
until the day these things shall take place."

[21]

When Zacharias finally came out from the Temple, the people realized that he was unable to speak. They knew he had seen a vision. Zacharias made signs to them and remained speechless.

When his time of service in the Temple was complete, Zacharias left Jerusalem and returned to his home. He was filled with great excitement over what the angel had told him and soon Elizabeth, too, understood the good news. She was overwhelmed with joy and gave thanks to God, saying:

"The Lord has done this thing for me.
He has taken away my disgrace among men."

For the next five months, Elizabeth remained in seclusion. It was during this time that Mary, her cousin, also with child, came to visit her.

And when the time of Elizabeth arrived, she gave birth to a son. The news of the arrival of the child spread to their neighbors and relatives. They rejoiced over the kindness that the Lord had shown and, on the eighth day after the birth, gathered for the naming of the child.

All who gathered presumed that the child would be named after his father and, indeed, had begun to call him Zacharias. But when Elizabeth heard this, she protested, saying:

"No, he shall be called John."

Everyone was surprised and said to Elizabeth:

"There is no one of your family
that is called by this name."

Then, using signs, they asked Zacharias what he wished his son to be called. Zacharias motioned for a writing tablet to be given him. On it he wrote:

"His name is John."

[22]

They all marveled at this and, at that moment, the mouth of Zacharias was opened and his tongue loosened, and he began to speak and praise God.

Zacharias then prophesied, saying:

"Blessed be the Lord of Israel, for He has
visited and redeemed His people.

"He has raised up a horn of salvation for us,
In the house of His servant, David.

"And you, John, shall be called the prophet
of the Most High.

"For you shall go before the Lord,
To prepare His way."

Word of these things soon spread throughout the countryside where Elizabeth and Zacharias lived. All who heard were fearful and wondered:

"What kind of child shall this be?"

The child, John, grew and matured in spirit and in the love of God.
He came to fulfill the prophecy of his father, as he spent
his life preaching about Jesus and baptizing
all who chose to follow
Him.

Mary and Joseph

MARY, A COUSIN OF Elizabeth, lived in Nazareth, a remote village in the back hills of southern Galilee. She was a gentle young woman, betrothed to a carpenter named Joseph, who also lived in Nazareth. Joseph was a kind, hardworking man who loved Mary very much.

One day, while Mary was sitting alone, the angel Gabriel appeared to her and said:

> *"Rejoice O highly favored daughter!*
> *The Lord is with you.*
> *Blessed are you among women."*

Mary was troubled by these words and wondered what this greeting could mean. Then the angel continued:

> *"Fear not, Mary, for you have found*
> *favor with God.*
>
> *"You shall bring forth a Son and shall*
> *give Him the Name Jesus.*
>
> *"He shall be great and shall be called the*
> *Son of the Most High.*
>
> *"The Lord God shall give Him the throne of*
> *His ancestor, David.*

The Shepherds and the Magi

NOW THERE WERE SHEPHERDS in the region keeping watch over their flocks by night. They were wondering about the great star, shining so brightly in the sky, when an angel of the Lord appeared to them. The shepherds were very much afraid, but the angel said to them:

"Be not afraid, for behold, I bring you
good tidings of great joy, which shall be
to all people.

"For there is born to you this day, in
the city of David, a Saviour Who
is Christ the Lord.

"And this is the sign unto you:
You shall find the Infant wrapped in
swaddling clothes and lying in a manger."

And suddenly there appeared in the heavens a multitude of angels praising God, saying:

"Glory to God in the highest, and on earth,
Peace to men of good will."

When the angels had returned to heaven, the shepherds said to one another:

[33]

*"Let us go over to Bethlehem and see this event
which the Lord has made known to us."*

So they went in haste to Bethlehem and found Mary and Joseph and the Baby, wrapped in swaddling clothes and lying in a manger, just as the angel had told them. They were astonished and knelt down in adoration, understanding all that had been said to them concerning this Child. They told all of this to Mary, who treasured it and reflected upon it in her heart.

The shepherds then went out and told the people of these wondrous things. All who heard were amazed at what they were told. The shepherds then returned to their flocks in the fields, glorifying and praising God for all that they had seen and heard.

The bright star was also seen in the East by three wise men, or Magi. They were Melchior from Persia, Gaspar from India and Balthasar from Arabia.*

The Magi followed the star to Jerusalem and there asked:

*"Where is the King of the Jews?
We have observed His star in the East
and have come to worship Him."*

At this news, Herod, the King of Palestine, became greatly disturbed. He summoned the chief priests and scribes of the people and asked of them where the Messiah was to be born. They replied:

*"In Bethlehem of Judea, for it is
so written by the prophet Micah."*

And the high priests related the prophecy to Herod:

---

*There is disagreement among scholars regarding the Magi. Some say there were 12, whereas others say there were only three. There is also controversy as to where they came from. Their names first appeared in writings of the eighth century.

"But you, Bethlehem in Ephrathah,
Though small among the clans of Judah,
From you shall come forth a Ruler,
One whose roots are from long past."

Herod called the Magi aside and asked them the exact time that the star had appeared. He then sent them to Bethlehem, telling them:

"Go and learn all that you may about the Child.
When you have found Him, bring me word again,
So that I also may go and adore Him."

And so the Magi set out for Bethlehem. Soon the great star, which they had originally seen in the East, reappeared. They were overjoyed to see the star and followed it until it stopped over the stable. The Magi entered and, seeing the Child with Mary, fell upon their knees and worshipped Him. Then they opened their treasures and presented Him with gifts of gold, frankincense and myrrh.

The Magi then returned to their own countries, but by a different route than they had come. For they had received a message in a dream, warning them of the evil intentions of Herod.

Jesus is Presented in the Temple

MARY AND JOSEPH, being faithful to their Hebrew religion, were careful to carry out the traditional laws pertaining to the birth of a child. These laws had been passed down from the Lord to Abraham and Moses. One of these laws stated that every male child must be circumcised and that this should be done when the child was eight days old. Another required that the first-born male be consecrated to the Lord. There was also a law that applied to the new mother, defining a period of time after birth for her purification. During this time, she was forbidden to touch anything sacred or to enter the Temple. The period of time was defined as 40 days if the child was male, or 80 days if it was female. When the purification period was over, the mother was then to take a lamb and a turtle dove to the Temple as sacrificial offerings. In practice, poor people frequently took two turtle doves or pigeons instead of the lamb.

And so, in adherence to the law, Joseph circumcised the Child when He was eight days old. Joseph and Mary gave Him the Name Jesus, as they had been instructed to do by the angel Gabriel. And, when 40 days had passed since the birth, and the purification period for Mary was complete, she and Joseph took Jesus and went to the Temple in Jerusalem for His consecration. They took with them two turtle doves as their offering for the purification of Mary.

Now there was living in Jerusalem at that time a man named Simeon. He was a just and devout man. The Holy Spirit had revealed to him that he would not die until he had seen the Messiah. On this day, when Mary and Joseph came to the Temple, Simeon also came, inspired by the Holy Spirit. When he saw the Child Jesus, he took Him in his arms and praised God saying:

[37]

*"Now, Lord, as You promised, You may
dismiss Your servant in peace. You have
fulfilled Your word.*

*"For my eyes have seen Your saving deed,
Displayed for all the people to see.*

*"A revealing light to the Gentiles,
The Glory of Your people, Israel."*

Mary and Joseph marveled at what Simeon said about Jesus. Simeon then blessed them and said to Mary:

*"This Child is destined to be the downfall
and rise of many in Israel,
A sign that will be opposed.*

*"And a sword shall pierce your own soul too,
So that the thoughts of many hearts
may be laid bare."*

There was also a prophetess named Anna in the Temple this day. Anna was 84 years old and had been a widow for many years. She was constant-ly in the Temple, worshipping day and night, fasting and praying. When Anna saw Jesus, she gave thanks to God. And afterwards, she announced to all who were looking forward to the redemption of Jerusalem that the Messiah had come.

[38]

The Return to Nazareth

K ING HEROD SOON REALIZED that he had been deceived by the Magi, for they had not returned to tell him where the Child was born as he had asked them to do. At this, he became greatly angered, for he feared the newborn King would someday take his throne. He therefore sent out an order that every male child, two years of age or younger in Bethlehem and nearby areas, be murdered.

When Herod sent out this order, an angel of the Lord appeared to Joseph in a dream and said to him:

> *"Arise, and take the Child and His mother and*
> *flee into Egypt. And you shall remain there*
> *until I bring you word. For Herod is seeking*
> *the Child to destroy Him."*

Joseph arose from his dream and that night took the Child and His mother and departed for Egypt. This took place so as to fulfill the prophecy of Hosea which said:

> *"Out of Egypt have I called My Son."*

They remained in Egypt until the death of Herod, when the angel of the Lord again appeared to Joseph in a dream saying:

> *"Arise and take the Child and His mother*
> *and go into the land of Israel.*

[39]

For those who sought the Child's life
are now dead."

Joseph did as the angel had ordered, and went into Israel with Mary and the Child. But when he heard that the Archelaus, the cruel son of Herod, now reigned over Judea, Joseph was afraid to go there. And, having been warned by God in a dream not to go into Judea, Joseph and Mary and Jesus returned to their home in Nazareth in Galilee by way of a route through Perea.

The Child Jesus grew in strength and wisdom, for the grace of God was upon Him.

When He was 12 years old, Mary and Joseph took Jesus to Jerusalem for the Hebrew feast of the Passover, as was their custom. When the Passover feast was complete, they joined a caravan of friends and relatives returning to Galilee. Mary and Joseph thought that Jesus was in the caravan with relatives. They did not realize that He had remained behind in Jerusalem. The caravan traveled nearly one full day before Mary and Joseph discovered that Jesus was not among their relatives. They then returned to Jerusalem to search for Him.

And it came to pass that, after three days of searching, Mary and Joseph found Jesus in the Temple. He was sitting in the midst of the teachers, listening to them and asking them questions. All those who heard Him were astonished at His wisdom and His answers.

When His parents saw Him, they were amazed. But Mary said to Jesus:

"Son, why have You treated us like this?
Behold, Your father and I have searched for You,
Sorrowing."

And Jesus said to them:

"Why have you searched for Me?
Do you not know that I must be
about My Father's business?"

[40]

Mary and Joseph did not understand what He said to them. But Jesus went with them and they returned to Nazareth. There, Jesus remained obedient to His parents and advanced in wisdom and grace before God and men.

In His early adulthood, Jesus worked as a carpenter, like Joseph. And when He was about 30 years old, He went from Nazareth to the River Jordan, where John was baptizing the people. As John baptized, he said to the people:

> *"I baptize you with water for the sake of*
> *repentance.*
>
> *"But One mightier then I, whose sandals I am*
> *not fit to undo,*
> *Shall baptize you with the Holy Spirit."*

When John saw Jesus approaching, he announced to the people:

> *"Behold the Lamb of God.*
> *Behold Him Who taketh away*
> *the sin of the world.*
> *This is He of Whom I have spoken."*

Then Jesus told John that He wished to be baptized. At first John refused, saying:

> *"I should be baptized by You.*
> *Yet, You come to me to be baptized."*

Jesus replied:

> *"Let it be so, for by us must the*
> *work of God be fulfilled."*

John relented and baptized Jesus. When the baptism was complete, the heavens opened and the Spirit of God descended upon Jesus. And, behold, a voice from heaven was heard saying:

"This is My beloved Son,
In Whom I am well pleased."

After this, John gave testimony:

"I saw the Spirit descend
like a dove from the sky.
And it came to rest upon Him.

"Now I have seen for myself.
This is the Son of God."

With His baptism, Jesus put aside His work as a carpenter and peaceful life with Mary and Joseph. For it was now time to begin the work of His Heavenly Father, the work that would lead to a painful crucifixion, a glorious resurrection and, through these, the redemption of mankind.

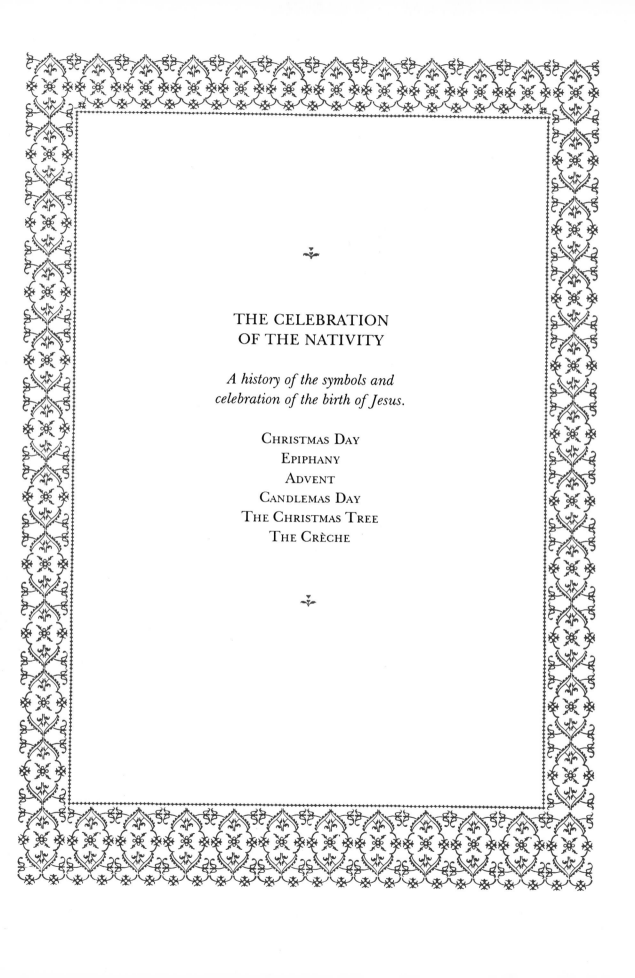

THE CELEBRATION
OF THE NATIVITY

*A history of the symbols and
celebration of the birth of Jesus.*

CHRISTMAS DAY
EPIPHANY
ADVENT
CANDLEMAS DAY
THE CHRISTMAS TREE
THE CRÈCHE

The Celebration of the Nativity

IT IS BELIEVED that a celebration honoring the Nativity of Jesus was instituted in Rome by Emperor Constantine the Great sometime before the year 336 AD. Constantine converted to Christianity in the year 312 and, following this conversion, initiated the evolution of the Roman Empire into a Christian state. Constantine was a committed Christian and built many churches and cathedrals. His mother, Helena, also a converted Christian, founded a church at the place of the Nativity in Bethlehem.

Prior to the adoption of Christianity, the people of the Roman Empire worshipped many pagan gods. Among these gods were Saturn and Mithra. Saturn was the god of agriculture. His great festival, the Saturnalia, was the most popular and merry of all Roman festivals. It was celebrated each winter from December 17 until December 24. During the festival, businesses, schools and courts of law were closed. Slaves were given temporary freedom to say and do what they wanted. People exchanged gifts and there was much feasting, dancing and other forms of celebration.

Mithra was worshipped by the Romans as the god of the sun. The festival in his honor was known as Dies Invicti Solis, or the Day of the Unconquered Sun. It was held on December 25, which was supposedly the birthday of Mithra as well as the first day of the ancient winter solstice which extended until January 6. The winter solstice is the period of time during the year when the days are shortest, due to the pattern of rotation of the earth around the sun. When the solstice is over, the days begin to get longer, heralding the coming of spring and the planting of crops. The festival of the Unconquered Sun therefore represented to the people the rebirth of the god of the sun and the renewal of life. This festival was, like Saturnalia, characterized by much feasting and merrymaking.

The Roman people were very attached to these pagan festivals. As they converted to Christianity, it was difficult for them to forsake the pleasures of these celebrations. And, since the exact date of the birth of Jesus was never recorded, the Church at Rome adopted December 25 as the official date of the Birth. The gift giving, feasting and merrymaking, previously associated with pagan gods, was continued, but now in honor of Jesus, the Messiah.

Sometime after this, but still in the fourth century, January 6 came to be celebrated as the Epiphany, or the Manifestation of Christ. The Epiphany, in the Western Church, commemorates the visit of the Magi, whereas in the Eastern Church, it commemorates the baptism of Jesus by John the Baptist.

Advent, once considered a period of fasting in preparation for the celebration of the birth of Jesus, was first instituted in Tours, France in the middle to late fifth century. Originally, Advent was a six-week period beginning on St. Martin's Day, November 11, and referred to as St. Martin's Lent. Sometime in the sixth century, Advent was adopted by Rome and the period was shortened to four weeks.

Candlemas Day, the festival commemorating the purification of Mary and the consecration of Jesus, was first known to be celebrated in Jerusalem in the late fourth century. Then, it was celebrated on February 14, 40 days after Epiphany. In 542, Justinian I, emperor of the Byzantine Empire, decreed that the date should be moved back to February 2, 40 days after the birth. The celebration of the festival was instituted in the Western Church sometime in the late seventh century. In the Eastern Church, this festival primarily celebrates Christ, while in the Western Church it celebrates the Virgin Mary. It is called Candlemas because of the custom of observing the festival with a procession of lighted candles.

It is not known how or when the celebration of the Nativity of Jesus came to be called "Christmas" in much of the world. However, the name is generally accepted as being of Old English derivation, *Cristes Maesse*, meaning "Mass of Christ." Today, there is an abundance of decorations and symbols that characterize the Christmas holiday.

By far, the most popular symbol of this holiday is the Christmas tree. The modern day Christmas tree most likely originated in western Germany. During the Middle Ages (500-1500), there was a popular miracle play called *Adam and Eve*, depicting events from the Bible. The main focus of the scenery for the play was a Paradise tree, a fir tree hung with apples, representing the Garden of Eden. Sometime in the 15th century, the German people began to display Paradise trees in their homes. These were set up on December 24, the religious feast day of Adam and Eve. Instead of apples, however, they were hung with wafers, symbolic of the Host. Eventually, the wafers were replaced by cookies of various shapes.

In addition to the Paradise tree, the German people also constructed Christmas pyramids in their homes. A pyramid was made up of a series of different-sized shelves, forming a triangle. On the shelves were placed figurines, candles and a star. By the 16th century, the Paradise tree and the Christmas pyramid had blended together to become the Christmas tree. The tradition of the Christmas tree was brought to the United States by German settlers as early as the 17th century. However, it was not until the 19th century that the Christmas tree became a fashionable part of the celebration throughout much of Europe and the United States.

Another symbol of the season, although not as universally popular as the Christmas tree, is the Nativity scene. The Nativity was depicted in religious art as early as the fourth century and remained an important part of it for many centuries. However, the Nativity scene as we know it today was first popularized by Saint Francis of Assisi in the year 1223 in Greccio, Italy. There, Saint Francis erected a manger scene, or *presèpio* as it is called in Italian, using live animals and people, except for the infant Christ Child, to represent the various participants at the birth of Jesus. This became an annual custom in Greccio and soon spread to other cities. Eventually people began putting up small Nativity scenes in their homes, using carved figurines. This custom became especially popular in Europe during the 17th and 18th centuries. The Nativity scene today is often referred to as a *crèche*, the French word for manger or crib.

[46]

Christmas is now the most widely celebrated and joyful holiday in the Western world. It is characterized by feasting, gift-giving, Christmas trees, crèches and Christmas caroling, just as it has been for centuries. Most of all, Christmas is a time of spiritual renewal, signaling new hope for mankind through the birth of the Messiah.

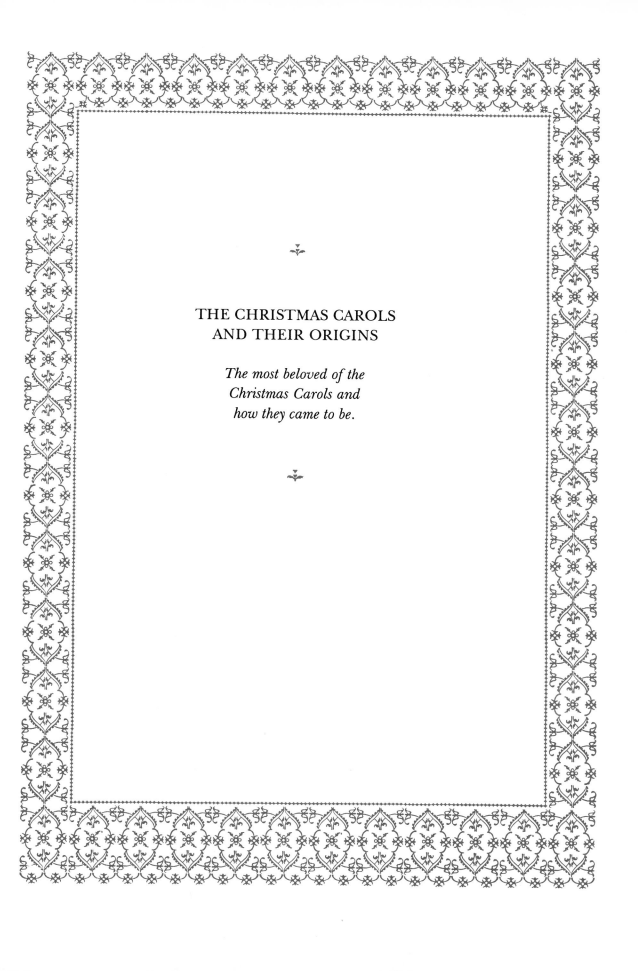

THE CHRISTMAS CAROLS
AND THEIR ORIGINS

*The most beloved of the
Christmas Carols and
how they came to be.*

Christmas Carols

Christmas Carols

THE WORD "CAROL" was used in early Medieval England to describe a song about any subject, written in a pattern of uniform verses, alternating with a refrain. But in the 14th century, carols were almost exclusively associated with religious subjects, such as the Virgin Mary, the Christ Child or the saints. During the Reformation, which spanned the 16th and 17th centuries, the religious carol essentially disappeared.

A revival of the religious carol began in England in the second half of the 18th century. During this revival, many old Christmas songs became popular again. Hundreds of new carols were also written and many foreign carols, especially those in French, were translated into English.

Many of the better known Christmas songs have English or French origins, and were written during or prior to the revival period. While many of them do not adhere to the traditional form of the carol, nonetheless, today all religious Christmas songs are popularly referred to as carols.

No religious or secular celebration has inspired more musical composition than has Christmas. The richness of the melodies, as well as the joyful spirit of the lyrics, have kept this music alive for centuries. Throughout the years, Christmas music has been rendered in both classical and popular modes. It has been performed by symphony orchestras and opera companies. It has also been performed by folk singers, pop singers and even rock-and-roll singers.

The Christmas carols give this season a special feeling of joy and gladness. They are expressions of hopeful hearts, echoing the dream of Peace on Earth and Good Will Toward Man.

[51]

Angels We Have Heard on High

TEXT - *18th Century* - Traditional French

MUSIC - *18th Century* - Traditional French

Both the author and composer of this carol are unknown. However, the music and the text are presumed to have originated in France in the 18th century. The refrain, "Gloria in Excelsis Deo," is Latin and means "Glory to God in the Highest." It is interesting that this refrain has always been sung in Latin. When the text was translated from French to English in London in 1862, the original Latin was retained.

The sweet simplicity of the music and words, combined with the contrasting style of the refrain, make this carol one that everyone enjoys singing.

Angels We Have Heard on High

Away in a Manger

Text -
Verses 1,2 - Anonymous
Verse 3 - 1905 - by John T. McFarland (1851-1913); American

Music - *1887* - by James R. Murray (1841-1905); American

The text for the original two verses of this carol was once thought to have been written by Martin Luther. However, studies now indicate that the text was likely written by an unknown author in Pennsylvania during the 19th century.

Around 1905, John McFarland, a Methodist minister and Secretary of the Methodist Board of Sunday Schools in New York, wrote the third verse. All three verses now generally appear with this carol.

James Murray wrote the music for this carol and published it in 1887 in a collection of songs titled *Dainty Songs for Little Lads and Lasses*. It is often referred to as a cradlesong or lullaby.

With its delicate melody and innocent words, this carol is especially lovely when rendered by the voices of young children.

[54]

Away in a Manger

1. A - way in a man - ger, no crib for a bed, The lit - tle Lord
2. The cat - tle are low - ing, the Ba - by a - wakes, But lit - tle Lord
3. Be near me, Lord Je - sus, I ask Thee to stay Close by me for -

Je - sus laid down His sweet head; The stars in the sky looked
Je - sus no cry - ing He makes. I love Thee, Lord Je - sus, look
ev - er, and love me, I pray. Bless all the dear chil - dren in

down where He lay, The lit - tle Lord Je - sus, a - sleep on the hay.
down from the sky, And stay by my cra - dle till morn - ing is nigh.
Thy ten - der care, And fit us for heav - en, to live with Thee there.

The First Noel

TEXT - Traditional English

MUSIC - Traditional English

ARRANGEMENT - *1871* - by Sir John Stainer (1840-1901); English

This carol is believed to be over three hundred years old and was originally a simple street song. While it is considered an English carol, it may have originated in France. The text and music first appeared in print in 1833, published in London by William Sandys in *Christmas Carols Ancient and Modern.*

The music, as it is sung today, was arranged by John Stainer, a noted English composer and organist. The arrangement was published by Stainer in 1871 in *Christmas Carols Old and New.*

Passed from generation to generation, this carol remains one of the musical highlights of the Christmas season.

The First Noel

1. The first No - el, the an - gel did say, Was to cer - tain poor
2. They look - ed up and saw a star Shin - ing in the
3. And by the light of that same star Three wise men
4. This star drew nigh to the north - west, O'er Beth - le -
5. Then en - tered in those wise men three, Full rev - 'rent -
6. Then let us all with one ac - cord Sing prais - es

shep - herds in fields as they lay; In fields where they lay
east, be - yond them far, And to the earth it
came from coun - try far; To seek for a king was
hem it took its rest, And there it did both
ly up - on their knee, And of - fered there in
to our heav'n - ly Lord, That hath made heav'n and

keep - ing their sheep, On a cold win - ter's night that was so deep.
gave great light, And so it con - tin - ued both day and night.
their in - tent, And to fol - low the star wher - ev - er it went.
stop and stay, Right o - ver the place where Je - sus lay.
His pres - ence Their gold, and myrrh, and frank - in - cense.
earth of naught, And with His blood man - kind hath bought.

Refrain

No - el, No - el, No - el, No - el,

Born is the King of Is - ra - el.

God Rest Ye Merry, Gentlemen

TEXT - *18th Century* - Traditional English

MUSIC - *18th Century* - Traditional English

This carol first appeared in 1770 in a collection of songs titled *Roxburgh Ballads*. It probably originated in London as a common street song. Little else is known about the history or authorship of this carol.

The first line of this carol, sometimes difficult to understand, means "Gentlemen, may God keep you in merry spirits." This line was used by Charles Dickens in *A Christmas Carol*. In this classic Christmas story, Ebenezer Scrooge becomes angry when he hears carolers sing this line and threatens them with a ruler.

Though this carol failed to cheer grumpy old Scrooge, its lively melody and words of "comfort and joy" always help to brighten the Christmas season.

[58]

God Rest Ye Merry, Gentlemen

Go Tell It on the Mountain

TEXT
Refrain - Traditional Negro Spiritual
Verses - by John W. Work, II (1901-1967); American

MUSIC - Traditional Negro Spiritual

The verses for this carol were written by a gifted composer, John Wesley Work, II, from Tullahoma, Tennessee. After graduating from Fisk University in 1923, Work continued his studies at Columbia University, Yale University and The Juilliard School of Music. In 1927, he returned to Fisk University, where, like his father, he served as professor of music and director of the famous Fisk Jubilee Singers. While at Fisk, Work also composed musical works for string orchestra and chorus as well as for folk singers. It was for the Jubilee Singers that Work wrote the verses for this carol.

The Jubilee Singers was formed in 1871 by a group of emancipated slaves. Also students at the newly founded Fisk University, the singers set out to raise funds for their college. Their concerts, filled with slave songs from their recent past, thrilled audiences in America as well as Europe. After only eight years of touring, the singers had raised enough money to pay for a new campus. They had also assured a place in musical history for the Negro spiritual.

"Go Tell It on the Mountain" is a fine example of a Negro spiritual. It is also a wonderful, vibrant Christmas carol.

[60]

Go Tell It on the Mountain

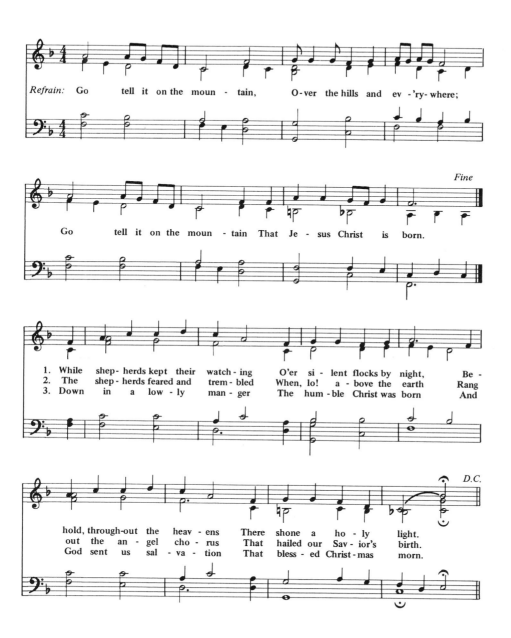

Refrain: Go tell it on the moun - tain, O - ver the hills and ev - 'ry - where;

Go tell it on the moun - tain That Je - sus Christ is born.

1. While shep- herds kept their watch - ing O'er si - lent flocks by night, Be -
2. The shep - herds feared and trem - bled When, lo! a - bove the earth Rang
3. Down in a low - ly man - ger The hum - ble Christ was born And

hold, through-out the heav - ens There shone a ho - ly light.
out the an - gel cho - rus That hailed our Sav - ior's birth.
God sent us sal - va - tion That bless - ed Christ - mas morn.

Hark the Herald Angels Sing

TEXT - *1738* - by Charles Wesley (1707-1788); English

MUSIC - *1840* - by Felix Mendelssohn (1809-1848); German

COMBINED - *1855* - by William Haymen Cummings; English

Charles Wesley, co-founder with his brother, John, of Methodism, wrote over 4,000 hymns, 50 of which are still in *The Methodist Hymnal*. He and Isaac Watts, author of "Joy to the World," were the most prolific hymn writers of all time. Wesley originally called this hymn poem "Hark, How All the Welkin Rings."

The music of Felix Mendelssohn is noted for its charm and elegance. Although he lived only a short time, Mendelssohn was very productive, composing many accomplished works before he was 20. The music for this carol is from the second movement, "God is Light," of a choral work titled "Festgesang" written to celebrate the four hundredth anniversary of the invention of the printing press by Gutenberg.

William Haymen Cummings, a tenor, realized how perfect the "Festgesang" arrangement was for Wesley's hymn. He combined the two and published the carol as it is known today.

The combined creativity of Mendelssohn and Wesley, both masters of their trades, make this carol more than a Christmas song. It is a musical work of art.

[62]

Hark the Herald Angels Sing

It Came Upon the Midnight Clear

Text - *1849* - by Edmund H. Sears (1810-1876); American

Music - *1849* - by Richard S. Willis (1819-1900); American

Edmund Sears, a Unitarian minister, was born in the Berkshire mountains of Massachusetts. He was educated at Union College and Harvard Divinity School and spent most of his life in the ministry in Wayland, Massachusetts. In addition to his ministry, Sears also did editorial work for the *Monthly Religious Magazine*. This poem was first published in 1850 in the *Christian Register* of Boston.

After graduating from Yale University, Richard Willis studied music in Germany under Felix Mendelssohn. Upon his return to the United States, he worked as a composer, a musical journalist and music critic for the New York *Tribune*. He also served as a vestryman at the Little Church Around the Corner in New York. Willis originally composed this music under the title "Christmas Carol." This music has frequently been used to accompany the carol "While Shepherds Watched Their Flocks by Night." It first appeared the same year as the poem of Edmund Sears, but it was not until some years later that this music and text were combined.

The pretty melody and poetic verses of this carol, repeating the angel's words to the shepherds of "Peace on Earth, Good Will to Men," especially symbolize the spirit of hope of the Christmas season.

It Came Upon the Midnight Clear

1. It came up-on the mid-night clear, That glo-rious song of old,
2. Still thru the clo-ven skies they come With peace-ful wings un-furled,
3. And ye, be-neath life's crush-ing load, Whose forms are bend-ing low,
4. For lo, the days are has-t'ning on, By proph-ets seen of old,

From an-gels bend-ing near the earth To touch their harps of gold:
And still their heav'n-ly mu-sic floats O'er all the wea-ry world:
Who toil a-long the climb-ing way With pain-ful steps and slow,
When with the ev-er-cir-cling years Shall come the time fore-told,

"Peace on the earth, good will to men, From heav'n's all-gra-cious King!"
A-bove its sad and low-ly plains They bend on hov-'ring wing,
Look now! for glad and gold-en hours Come swift-ly on the wing:
When the new heav'n and earth shall own The Prince of Peace their King,

The world in sol-emn still-ness lay To hear the an-gels sing.
And ev-er o'er its Ba-bel sounds The bless-ed an-gels sing.
O rest be-side the wea-ry road And hear the an-gels sing.
And the whole world send back the song Which now the an-gels sing.

Joy to the World

TEXT - *1719* - by Issac Watts (1674-1748); English

MUSIC - *1741* - by George F. Handel (1685-1759); German

ARRANGEMENT - *1839* - by Lowell Mason (1792-1872); American

Issac Watts was an English Nonconformist minister. He is regarded as the father of English hymnody, having written over 600 hymns. He also published 52 works of prose and poetry. Watts and John Wesley, author of "Hark! the Herald Angels Sing," were the most prolific of the English hymn writers.

George F. Handel is considered one of the greatest composers of the Baroque era. He wrote some of the most wonderful operatic, choral and sacred compositions of all time. One of his best known compositions, "The Messiah," is the source of the music for this carol.

"The Messiah," a narrative on the life of Jesus, was masterfully composed by Handel in only 23 days in 1741. It was first performed the following year in Dublin, Ireland. Two themes from this magnificent work, "Lift Up Your Hearts" and "Comfort Ye," comprise the music for this carol.

"Joy to the World," when sung by a full chorus and accompanied by orchestra, is truly thrilling to hear.

[66]

Joy to the World

O Come All Ye Faithful

Text - *1744* - by John F. Wade (1711-1786); English

Translation - *1841* - by Frederick Oakeley (1802-1880);   English

Music - *1744* - by John F. Wade

This carol was originally written in Latin and titled "Adéste Fidéles." For many years, the author was unknown. But a study published in 1947 credited authorship to John F. Wade.

Wade was an Englishman who worked in France as a copyist, compiling musical works for various Catholic organizations. This carol was first published as part of a collection of hymns compiled for the Catholic College in Lisbon, Portugal. That is why some hymnals refer to this carol as a Portuguese hymn.

In 1841, Frederick Oakeley, an English canon, translated the Latin text to English. The English version was later published in *Murray's Hymnal* in 1852. However, it is still often sung in the original Latin form.

Regardless of the language in which this carol is sung, the spirit of it is always exuberant and joyful.

LATIN VERSE
Adéste fidélis, laéti trumphántes,
Veníte, veníte in Béthlehem.
Natum vidéte, Regem angelórum.
Veníte adorémus, veníte adorémus,
Veníte adorémus, Dóminum.

O Come All Ye Faithful

O Come, O Come, Emmanuel

TEXT - *9th Century* - Latin

TRANSLATION - *1851* - by John M. Neale (1818-1866); English

MUSIC - *1854* - adopted by Thomas Helmore (1811-1890)

The structure and words of this carol date back to the 9th century. It was originally sung in Latin in Medieval monasteries during the Advent season. On each of seven successive nights, beginning on December 17, the Abbot of the Monastery and the monks would chant one of the seven verses, or antiphons as they are often referred to in liturgical music. Each verse spoke of a different aspect of Christ, upon which the monks could reflect that evening.

The original Latin text was translated to English by John M. Neale, one of the most noted translators of his time. The musical arrangement was adapted by Thomas Helmore from a hymn titled "Veni, Veni, Emmanuel."

This carol, unlike most others, does not celebrate the actual birth of Jesus. Rather, if one listens carefully, the voices of monks in ancient monasteries may be heard celebrating what the coming of Christ would mean to the world.

O Come, O Come, Emmanuel

O come, O come, Thou Lord of might,
Who to Thy tribes of Sinai's height;
In ancient times didst give the law,
In cloud and majesty and awe.

O come, O come, thou rod of Jesse's stem,
From every foe deliver them;

That trust thy mighty power to save,
And give them victory over the grave.

O come, thou key of David come,
And open wide our heavenly home;
Make safe the way that leads on high,
And close the path of misery.

Silent Night

TEXT - *1818* - by Joseph Mohr (1792-1849); Austrian

TRANSLATION - *1863* - by John F. Young (1820-1885); Austrian

MUSIC - *1818* - by Franz Gruber (1787-1863); German

Joseph Mohr was born in Salzburg, Austria and ordained a Roman Catholic priest in 1815. One Christmas eve in 1818, while serving as assistant pastor of the church of St. Nicholas in Oberndorf, Austria, Mohr felt inspired to write a new hymn for the Christmas service. Upon completion of the hymn, he asked the church organist, Franz Gruber, to set the words to music.

Gruber completed the music in time for the Christmas service. However, the church organ was broken, and so the carol was first rendered by Mohr and Gruber accompanied by a single guitar. Sometime later, when the organ was being repaired, Gruber played this carol on it to test out the tone. The organ repairman was moved by the song and took a copy back to his home in Zellerthal, Austria. There, he passed it on to a merchant, whose four daughters traveled with a touring group of singers. These girls sang the carol wherever they went and popularized it throughout Austria and Germany.

This carol has been translated into over 70 languages. John Young, bishop of the Episcopal Diocese of Florida, translated it from German to English.

The most serene and lovely of all the Christmas carols, "Silent Night", is probably also the most popular.

Silent Night

We Three Kings

TEXT - *1857* - John H. Hopkins (1820-1891); American

MUSIC - *1857* - by John H. Hopkins

This is one of the few Christmas carols where both music and text were written by the same person. John Hopkins, born in 1820 in Pittsburgh, Pennsylvania was a reporter for the New York *Courier and Enquirer* before being ordained an Episcopalian minister in 1850. Following his ordination, he served as instructor in charge of music at the New York Theological Seminary in New York City, and then as rector of Christ Church in Williamsport, Pennsylvania.

This carol was written while Hopkins was serving at the New York Theological Seminary. There, in 1857, he presented an elaborate Christmas pageant for which he composed all of the musical works. "We Three Kings" was one of the carols written for this pageant.

Hopkins wrote many other hymns and songs and published a book, *Carols, Hymns and Songs* in 1882. However, "We Three Kings" is his best known work and is considered a fine example of the American style of carol.

We Three Kings

1. We three kings of O - ri - ent are:
2. Born a King on Beth - le - hem's plain:
3. Frank - in - cense to of - fer have I:
4. Myrrh is mine: its bit - ter per - fume
5. Glo - rious now be - hold Him a - rise:

Bear - ing gifts we trav - erse a - far— Field and foun - tain,
Gold I bring to crown Him a - gain, King for - ev - er,
In - cense owns a De - i - ty nigh; Prayer and prais - ing,
Breathes a life of gath - er - ing gloom— Sor - r'wing, sigh - ing,
King and God and Sac - ri - fice; Al - le - lu - ia,

moor and moun - tain— Fol - low - ing yon - der star.
ceas - ing nev - er O - ver us all to reign.
all men rais - ing, Wor - ship Him, God on high.
bleed - ing, dy - ing, Sealed in the stone - cold tomb.
Al - le - lu - ia! Earth to heav'n re - plies.

Refrain

O star of won - der, star of night, Star with roy - al beau - ty bright,

West - ward lead - ing, still pro - ceed - ing, Guide us to thy per - fect light.

What Child is This?

Text - *1865* - by William C. Dix (1837-1898); English

Music - from Greensleeves, Traditional English Melody

The text for this carol is derived from a Christmas poem, "The Manger Throne," written by William Dix in 1865. Dix, born in Bristol, England, was the author of scores of hymns, many of which are still used. The inspiration for this text was the Gospel of Matthew, 2:1-12.

The music is from the traditional English folk melody, "Greensleeves." This melody dates back to the late 16th century, and has appeared with a variety of texts. It has been used for love songs, political ballads, waltzes and Christmas carols.

The pleasant, lilting strains of this classic melody, complimenting the charming simplicity of the verses, make this carol especially appealing.

What Child is This?

While Shepherds Watched
Their Flocks by Night

TEXT - *1708* - by Nahum Tate (1652-1715); Irish

MUSIC - *1728* - by George F. Handel (1685-1759); German

Nahum Tate was born in Dublin, Ireland, the son of an Irish clergyman. He graduated from the University of Dublin, after which he settled in London and embarked upon a literary career. There, he gained a fine reputation as a poet, publishing several volumes of verse. He was named Poet Laureate in 1692.

The text for this carol was published by Tate in 1700 as part of a collection of sixteen hymns titled *A Supplement to the New Version of the Psalms*. It was inspired by verses from the second chapter of the Gospel of Luke.

The music is from the closing aria, ACT II, of the opera "Siroë, King of Persia" by Handel. The musical adaption of this opera, from which the melody for this carol is derived, first appeared in 1815 as the melody for a hymn titled "Melodia Sacra." Handel also wrote the music for the carol "Joy to the World."

This carol, more than any other, accurately presents the Gospel message about the birth of Jesus in a beautifully, poetic manner.

While Shepherds Watched
Their Flocks by Night

1. While shep - herds watched their flocks by night, All
2. "Fear not!" said he; for might - y dread Had
3. "To you, in Da - vid's town this day, Is
4. "The heav'n - ly Babe you there shall find To
5. "All glo - ry be to God on high, And

seat - ed on the ground, The an - gel of the
seized their troub - led mind, "Glad ti - dings of great
born of Da - vid's line, The Sav - ior who is
hu - man view dis - played, All mean - ly wrapped in
to the earth be peace: Good will hence - forth from

Lord came down, And glo - ry shone a -
joy I bring To you and all man -
Christ the Lord, And this shall be the
swath - ing bands, And in a man - ger
heav'n to men, Be - gin and nev - er

round, And glo - ry shone a - round.
kind, To you and all man - kind.
sign: And this shall be the sign:
laid; And in a man - ger laid.
cease, Be - gin and nev - er cease."

O Holy Night

TEXT - by Cappeau de Roquemaure; French

TRANSLATION - by John S. Dwight (1813-1893); American

MUSIC - by Adolphe Adam (1803-1856); French

Although there is not much known about the author, or when the words or music for this carol were written, it is believed to have been popular in France in 1870. For there is an often repeated story that tells of an incident that occurred on Christmas eve of that year during the Franco-Prussian War. The French and German troops were ready for battle when suddenly a young French soldier stepped out and began singing "Cantique de Noel," the French title for this carol. In response, a German soldier came forward, singing a German carol. Not a shot was fired that evening.

Adolphe Adam was a noted composer of music for ballet and opera. His most famous works include the ballet "Giselle" (1841) and the operas "Le Postillon de Longjumeau" (1836) and "Giralda" (1850).

John Dwight, who translated the carol from French to English, was an ordained Unitarian minister. He later left the ministry to pursue a career as a musical journalist and critic, establishing *Dwight's Journal of Music* in 1852.

"O Holy Night," when sung by a good solo voice, is surely the most exhilarating of all the Christmas carols.

O Holy Night

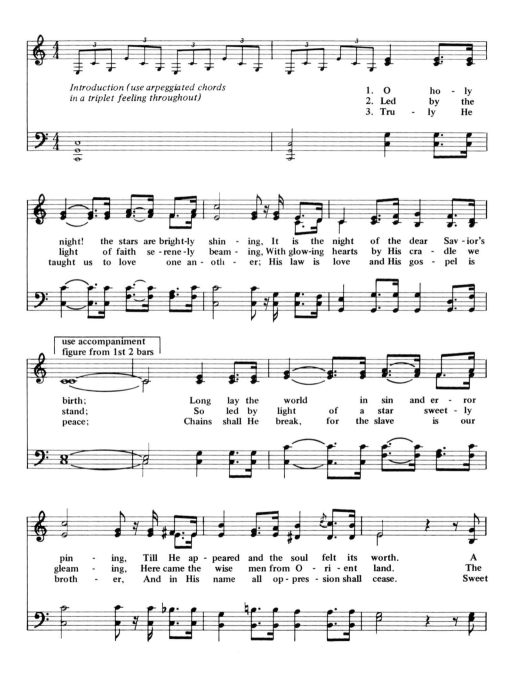

Introduction (use arpeggiated chords in a triplet feeling throughout)

1. O ho - ly
2. Led by the
3. Tru - ly He

night! the stars are bright-ly shin - ing, It is the night of the dear Sav - ior's
light of faith se - rene-ly beam - ing, With glow-ing hearts by His cra - dle we
taught us to love one an - oth - er; His law is love and His gos - pel is

use accompaniment figure from 1st 2 bars

birth; Long lay the world in sin and er - ror
stand; So led by light of a star sweet - ly
peace; Chains shall He break, for the slave is our

pin - ing, Till He ap - peared and the soul felt its worth. A
gleam - ing, Here came the wise men from O - ri - ent land. The
broth - er, And in His name all op - pres - sion shall cease. Sweet

thrill of hope the wear - y world re - joic - es, For yon - der breaks a
King of kings lay thus in low - ly man - ger, In all our tri - als
hymns of joy in grate-ful chor - us raise we, Let all with - in us

new and glo -rious morn; Fall on your knees, Oh,
born to be our Friend; He knows our need, To our
praise His ho - ly name; Christ is the Lord, Oh,

hear the an - gel voic - es! O night di -
weak - ness is no strang - er. Be - hold your
praise His name for - ev - er! His pow'r and

vine, O night when Christ was born!
King, be - fore Him low - ly bend!
glo - ry ev - er - more pro - claim!

cued notes opt. on last refrain

O night, O ho - ly night, O night di - vine!
Be - hold your King, be - fore Him low - ly bend!
His pow'r and glo - ry ev - er - more pro -claim!

BIBLES REFERENCED

The Holy Bible—Authorized King James Version
Collins' Clear Type Press
London and New York

The New English Bible
Oxford University Press
Cambridge University Press
1970

The Children's Bible
Golden Press—New York
Western Publishing Company, Inc.
Racine, Wisconsin

The Ryrie Study Bible
New American Standard Translation
Charles Caldwell Ryrie Th.D.,Ph.D.
Moody Press
Chicago, Illinois

The Life Application Bible
Tyndale House Publishers
Wheaton, Illinois

The New American Bible
Memorial Bibles International, Inc.
Box 23304 Nashville, TN 37202
(Confraternity of Christian Doctrine)

The Holy Bible with Crudens Complete Concordance
Henry S. Goodspeed & Co.
New York, NY - No. 180 Cherry St.
Cincinnati, OH - No. 195 West Fifth St.
Chicago, Ill.
1872,l 1873, 1875, 1877 - Copyright Data

The Way
(An edition of the Living Bible)
Tyndale House Publishers
Wheaton, Illinois

Other References

Saint Andrew Missal
The E.M. Lohmann Co.
Saint Paul, Minn.

Josephus The Jewish War
Penguin Books

The Life of Jesus
Grove Press Inc.

Harper's World of the New Testament
Harper & Row
San Francisco, CA

Encyclopedia Brittancia

Encyclopedia Americana

A Treasury of Christmas Songs and Carols
Houghton Mifflin Company
Boston, Mass. (1973)

The Christmas Book
McAfee Books
New York, NY

The Hymns and Hymn Writers of the Church
The Methodist Book Concern
New York, NY
Cincinnati, OH

Archaelolgy of the Bible: Book by Book
Harper & Row
San Francisco. CA

The Bible Knowledge Commentary
New Testament
John F. Walvoord
Roy B. Zuck
Victor Books
Wheaton, Illinois

The Bible Knowledge Commentary
Old Testament
John F. Walvoord
Roy B. Zuck
Victor Books
Wheaton, Illinois